for Advent and th

# SACRED SPACE

November 30, 2025 to January 10, 2026

from the website www.sacredspace.ie
**Prayer from the Irish Jesuits**

LOYOLA PRESS.
A JESUIT MINISTRY

LOYOLA PRESS.
A JESUIT MINISTRY

www.loyolapress.com

Copyright © by The Irish Jesuits 2025

This edition of *Sacred Space Advent Book* is published by arrangement with Messenger Publications, 37 Lower Leeson Street, Dublin D02 W938, Ireland.

Scripture quotations are from the *New Revised Standard Version Bible: Anglicised Catholic Edition*, copyright © 1989, 1993 National Council of the Churches of Christ in the United States of America. Used by permission. All rights reserved.

Loyola Press in Chicago thanks the Irish Jesuits and Messenger Press for preparing this book for publication.

Cover art credit: Yifei Fang/Moment/Getty Images

ISBN: 978-0-8294-5999-9

Published in Chicago, IL
Printed in Canada.
25 26 27 28 29 MQS 10 9 8 7 6 5 4 3 2 1

# Contents

# The Presence of God

Bless all who worship you, almighty God,
from the rising of the sun to its setting;
from your goodness enrich us,
by your love inspire us,
by your Spirit guide us,
by your power protect us,
in your mercy receive us,
now and always.

*Something to think and pray about each day this week:*

For us, in this Advent season, we are being called to realise that the tidy soul, like the tidy house, has to be worked at. It doesn't just happen. If we truly want the Lord to come and stay a while, we have to prepare the way. It's about putting the house in order—the soul in order. Somewhere and somehow we need to hear the centurion's words again and realise his words are ours too, 'Lord, I am not worthy to have you under my roof'. For that, we need a plan of action, a road map of sorts, to guide us on the journey.

The Sacrament of Reconciliation supplies some of that road map. Its coordinates are already there for us, and the initial movement might be found in 'Bless me Father, for I have sinned'.

Vincent Sherlock,
*Let Advent Be Advent*

**The Presence of God**

'I am standing at the door, knocking,' says the Lord. What a wonderful privilege that the Lord of all creation desires to come to me. I welcome his presence.

**Freedom**

Leave me here freely all alone. / In cell where never sunlight shone. / Should no one ever speak to me. / This golden silence makes me free!

> —Part of a poem written by a prisoner at Dachau concentration camp

**Consciousness**

How am I really feeling? Lighthearted? Heavyhearted? I may be very much at peace, happy to be here.

Equally, I may be frustrated, worried or angry.

I acknowledge how I really am. It is the real me whom the Lord loves.

**The Word**

I take my time to read the word of God slowly a few times, allowing myself to dwell on anything that strikes me. *(Please turn to the Scripture on the following pages. Inspiration points are there, should you need them. When you are ready, return here to continue.)*

**Conversation**
Do I notice myself reacting as I pray with the word of God? Do I feel challenged, comforted, angry? Imagining Jesus sitting or standing by me, I speak out my feelings, as one trusted friend to another.

**Conclusion**
Glory be to the Father, and to the Son, and to the Holy Spirit,
As it was in the beginning, is now and ever shall be,
World without end. Amen.

## Sunday 30 November
## First Sunday of Advent
*Matthew 24:37–44*

Jesus said to his disciples: 'For as the days of Noah were, so will be the coming of the Son of Man. For as in those days before the flood they were eating and drinking, marrying and giving in marriage, until the day Noah entered the ark, and they knew nothing until the flood came and swept them all away, so too will be the coming of the Son of Man. Then two will be in the field; one will be taken and one will be left. Two women will be grinding meal together; one will be taken and one will be left. Keep awake therefore, for you do not know on what day your Lord is coming. But understand this: if the owner of the house had known in what part of the night the thief was coming, he would have stayed awake and would not have let his house be broken into. Therefore you also must be ready, for the Son of Man is coming at an unexpected hour.'

• These early Gospel readings of Advent encourage us to stay awake and alert. In reality for me this might mean that I will try to notice anything that has struck me in my daily living for the past few days. I may recall a conversation with a friend, or an event that—if I stay with it—may have something to say to me. Could this possibly be God speaking to me? How else would I expect the Lord to interact with me?

## Monday 1 December
*Matthew 8:5–11*

When he entered Capernaum, a centurion came to him, appealing to him and saying, 'Lord, my servant is lying at home paralysed, in terrible distress.' And he said to him, 'I will come and cure him.' The centurion answered, 'Lord, I am not worthy to have you come under my roof; but only speak the word, and my servant will be healed. For I also am a man under authority, with soldiers under me; and I say to one, "Go", and he goes, and to another, "Come", and he comes, and to my slave, "Do this", and the slave does it.' When Jesus heard him, he was amazed and said to those who followed him, 'Truly I tell you, in no one in Israel have I found such faith. I tell you, many will come from east and west and will eat with Abraham and Isaac and Jacob in the kingdom of heaven.'

• In today's Scripture we try to take courage from the figure of the centurion who takes his courage in his hands and asks Jesus for faith and energy as he seeks relief and assistance in his attempts to help his servant escape from his terrible distress. We hope that we might have some of the same zeal as we set out on our Advent faith odyssey.

## Tuesday 2 December
*Luke 10:21–24*

At that same hour Jesus rejoiced in the Holy Spirit and said, 'I thank you, Father, Lord of heaven and earth, because you have hidden these things from the wise and the intelligent and have revealed them to infants; yes, Father, for such was your gracious will. All things have been handed over to me by my Father; and no one knows who the Son is except the Father, or who the Father is except the Son and anyone to whom the Son chooses to reveal him.' Then turning to the disciples, Jesus said to them privately, 'Blessed are the eyes that see what you see! For I tell you that many prophets and kings desired to see what you see, but did not see it, and to hear what you hear, but did not hear it.'

- Jesus himself seemed to be very conscious of the near presence of the Spirit in his life. We're told that the Spirit is sent to us at Confirmation, but are we at all aware of the Spirit gifting us with insights? Could I take a few minutes out and ask the Holy Spirit to come to my aid, sharpening my ability to notice how the presence and the influence of the Spirit affects me?

## Wednesday 3 December
*Matthew 15:29–37*

After Jesus had left that place, he passed along the Sea of Galilee, and he went up the mountain, where he sat down. Great crowds came to him, bringing with them the lame, the maimed, the blind, the mute, and many others. They put them at his feet, and he cured them, so that the crowd was amazed when they saw the mute speaking, the maimed whole, the lame walking, and the blind seeing. And they praised the God of Israel.

Then Jesus called his disciples to him and said, 'I have compassion for the crowd, because they have been with me now for three days and have nothing to eat; and I do not want to send them away hungry, for they might faint on the way.' The disciples said to him, 'Where are we to get enough bread in the desert to feed so great a crowd?' Jesus asked them, 'How many loaves have you?' They said, 'Seven, and a few small fish.' Then ordering the crowd to sit down on the ground, he took the seven loaves and the fish; and after giving thanks he broke them and gave them to the disciples, and the disciples gave them to the crowds. And all of them ate and were filled; and they took up the broken pieces left over, seven baskets full.

- The disciples seem to lose heart very easily when things are not working for them as they might wish. They can only spot the downside of today's scene. Jesus takes a completely different approach. He notes that the onlookers today must be tired and hungry.

- Jesus' question to his own disciples is 'What might we to do to encourage and inspire?', rather than 'What elements of the situation are likely to defeat us?'

## Thursday 4 December
### Matthew 7:21, 24–27

Jesus said to his disciples, 'Not everyone who says to me, "Lord, Lord", will enter the kingdom of heaven, but only one who does the will of my Father in heaven. . . . Everyone then who hears these words of mine and acts on them will be like a wise man who built his house on rock. The rain fell, the floods came, and the winds blew and beat on that house, but it did not fall, because it had been founded on rock. And everyone who hears these words of mine and does not act on them will be like a foolish man who built his house on sand. The rain fell, and the floods came, and the winds blew and beat against that house, and it fell—and great was its fall!'

- Jesus makes a distinction between two different types of listening—a listening that produces action and something positive, and a listening that brings forth nothing really constructive. He encourages us to make sure our listening brings forth something really worthwhile. Listening actively will help us understand what God has in mind for us and will shape our way of life.

- Are my eyes and ears continually open and alert and picking up moments and occasions when Jesus himself may be very close at hand? As the old motto goes, 'If you miss it . . . you miss it.'

## Friday 5 December
*Matthew 9:27–31*

As Jesus went on from there, two blind men followed him, crying loudly, 'Have mercy on us, Son of David!' When he entered the house, the blind men came to him; and Jesus said to them, 'Do you believe that I am able to do this?' They said to him, 'Yes, Lord.' Then he touched their eyes and said, 'According to your faith let it be done to you.' And their eyes were opened. Then Jesus sternly ordered them, 'See that no one knows of this.' But they went away and spread the news about him throughout that district.

- Two blind men have followed Jesus, and they make their intentions fairly plain, even though—being blind—they must have found it hard to keep in close contact. We ourselves cannot see Jesus with our physical eyes, yet we follow him. As often seems to be the case, the men's belief that Jesus in his goodness would do something worthwhile for them seems fairly clear, but Jesus gets them to spell out their trust and faith. When we make some request ourselves, is our sense of belief equally evident?

## Saturday 6 December
### Matthew 9:35–10:1, 5–8

Then Jesus went about all the cities and villages, teaching in their synagogues, and proclaiming the good news of the kingdom, and curing every disease and every sickness. When he saw the crowds, he had compassion for them, because they were harassed and helpless, like sheep without a shepherd. Then he said to his disciples, 'The harvest is plentiful, but the labourers are few; therefore ask the Lord of the harvest to send out labourers into his harvest.' Then Jesus summoned his twelve disciples and gave them authority over unclean spirits, to cast them out, and to cure every disease and every sickness. . . . These twelve Jesus sent out with the following instructions:

'Go nowhere among the Gentiles, and enter no town of the Samaritans, but go rather to the lost sheep of the house of Israel. As you go, proclaim the good news, "The kingdom of heaven has come near." Cure the sick, raise the dead, cleanse the lepers, cast out demons. You received without payment; give without payment.'

- I try to get a sense of what it must have been like to move around with Jesus on a daily basis. He must have been encouraged as he noticed the crowds getting bigger and more enthusiastic. He didn't spare himself. Perhaps I could strive to be similarly selfless as I go about my day.

*Something to think and pray about each day this week:*

Over time, our images of Mary have become rather sanitised, partly due to cultural perceptions of the role of women but also due to the longstanding correlation in Church tradition between 'holiness' and 'purity' for women.

We return to Mary's roots, to her early appearance as the brave, decisive, breathless, excited young woman who rushed to Elizabeth's house, pregnant with God's promise, pregnant with joy, carrying the Word of God, passing it on. Many of us have a particular devotion to Mary. Advent is an ideal time to reflect on what Mary can teach us about being a disciple and 'God-bearer' (*Theotokos*). God asks each of us to be bearers of his love and his Word. Our challenge is to create a space for God in all of our human experience, in our joy and our brokenness. Let us follow in the footsteps of the first evangelist, Mary. Let us also listen to the experiences of the women in our

Church and society who, through their strength and enthusiasm, continue the task of carrying Christ in and to the world.

Tríona Doherty and Jane Mellett,
*The Deep End:*
*A Journey with the Sunday Gospels in the Year of Luke*

## The Presence of God

'Be still, and know that I am God!' Lord, may your spirit guide me to seek your loving presence more and more, for it is there I find rest and refreshment from this busy world.

## Freedom

By God's grace I was born to live in freedom. Free to enjoy the pleasures he created for me. Dear Lord, grant that I may live as you intended, with complete confidence in your loving care.

## Consciousness

How am I today? Where am I with God? With others? Do I have something to be grateful for? Then I give thanks. Is there something I am sorry for? Then I ask forgiveness.

## The Word

God speaks to each of us individually. I need to listen, to hear what he is saying to me. Read the text a few times, then listen. *(Please turn to the Scripture on the following pages. Inspiration points are there, should you need them. When you are ready, return here to continue.)*

## Conversation

How has God's word moved me? Has it left me cold? Has it consoled me or moved me to act in a new way? I imagine Jesus standing or sitting beside me. I turn and share my feelings with him.

**Conclusion**

I thank God for these moments we have spent together and for any insights I have been given concerning the text.

## Sunday 7 December
## Second Sunday of Advent
*Matthew 3:1–12*

In those days John the Baptist appeared in the wilderness of Judea, proclaiming, 'Repent, for the kingdom of heaven has come near.' This is the one of whom the prophet Isaiah spoke when he said,

> 'The voice of one crying out in the wilderness:
> "Prepare the way of the Lord,
>      make his paths straight."'

Now John wore clothing of camel's hair with a leather belt around his waist, and his food was locusts and wild honey. Then the people of Jerusalem and all Judea were going out to him, and all the region along the Jordan, and they were baptised by him in the river Jordan, confessing their sins.

But when he saw many Pharisees and Sadducees coming for baptism, he said to them, 'You brood of vipers! Who warned you to flee from the wrath to come? Bear fruit worthy of repentance. Do not presume to say to yourselves, "We have Abraham as our ancestor"; for I tell you, God is able from these stones to raise up children to Abraham. Even now the axe is lying at the root of the trees; every tree therefore that does not bear good fruit is cut down and thrown into the fire.

'I baptise you with water for repentance, but one who is more powerful than I is coming after me; I am not worthy to carry his sandals. He will baptise you with the Holy Spirit and fire. His winnowing-fork is in his hand, and he will clear his threshing-floor and will gather his wheat into the granary; but the chaff he will burn with unquenchable fire.'

- Today we find John the Baptist playing a central role in the scene we're contemplating. He has appeared in the wilderness, and clearly people are beginning both to hear about him and to be very struck by what he has to say. His message today might be summed up in just one of his sentences—'Prepare the way of the Lord'.

- To proclaim and make clear this point, John constantly turned the light away from himself. You might be struck by his selfless behaviour and the fact that he wasn't prepared to sugar-coat what he felt he had been sent to say. He comes straight to the point, and insists on the fact that his followers should look beyond whatever he has to offer and give their allegiance to the Saviour rather than to himself.

# Monday 8 December
# The Immaculate Conception of the BVM
*Luke 1:26–38*

In the sixth month the angel Gabriel was sent by God to a town in Galilee called Nazareth, to a virgin engaged to a man whose name was Joseph, of the house of David. The virgin's name was Mary. And he came to her and said, 'Greetings, favoured one! The Lord is with you.' But she was much perplexed by his words and pondered what sort of greeting this might be. The angel said to her, 'Do not be afraid, Mary, for you have found favour with God. And now, you will conceive in your womb and bear a son, and you will name him Jesus. He will be great, and will be called the Son of the Most High, and the Lord God will give to him the throne of his ancestor David. He will reign over the house of Jacob for ever, and of his kingdom there will be no end.' Mary said to the angel, 'How can this be, since I am a virgin?' The angel said to her, 'The Holy Spirit will come upon you, and the power of the Most High will overshadow you; therefore the child to be born will be holy; he will be called Son of God. And now, your relative Elizabeth in her old age has also conceived a son; and this is the sixth month for her who was said to be barren. For nothing will be impossible with God.' Then Mary said, 'Here am I, the servant of the Lord; let it be with me according to your word.' Then the angel departed from her.

- We are at a key moment in God's dealings with humanity. So much would hang on how Mary responded to the angel's invitation. We try to get into the scene itself, making ourselves part of it, imagining the moment when Gabriel suddenly appears. It must have been stunning and frightening for Mary, but her generosity of spirit dictated her response. 'Yes' was the word that came automatically to her lips, even if what that 'Yes' might mean was still something of a mystery to her. She surrendered with open arms to the path God laid out for her.

## Tuesday 9 December
*Matthew 18:12–14*

Jesus said to his disciples, 'What do you think? If a shepherd has a hundred sheep, and one of them has gone astray, does he not leave the ninety-nine on the mountains and go in search of the one that went astray? And if he finds it, truly I tell you, he rejoices over it more than over the ninety-nine that never went astray. So it is not the will of your Father in heaven that one of these little ones should be lost.'

- Which point do you think would have stirred the hearts of the disciples? Pause for a moment and ask Jesus to help you discern which aspect of the image is touching you. Is it the point about Jesus always seeming to have a mind for the weakest around him, or that those who are in trouble usually seem to be treated with great gentleness? Could it be me, Lord, on whom you have your best attention settled at this very moment?

## Wednesday 10 December
### Matthew 11:28–30

Jesus said, 'Come to me, all you that are weary and are carrying heavy burdens, and I will give you rest. Take my yoke upon you, and learn from me; for I am gentle and humble in heart, and you will find rest for your souls. For my yoke is easy, and my burden is light.'

- In the passage we are presented with today, Jesus seems much more inclusive than seems to have been generally the case in first-century Palestine. All who are weary—not just those who are powerful, or male, or who hold powerful positions—are invited and urged to come to him. To all who seek it, peace and rest will be given.

- I ask for the confidence I need, Lord, to follow through on your invitation and believe in your offer.

## Thursday 11 December
*Matthew 11:11–15*

Jesus said to the crowds, 'Truly I tell you, among those born of women no one has arisen greater than John the Baptist; yet the least in the kingdom of heaven is greater than he. From the days of John the Baptist until now the kingdom of heaven has suffered violence, and the violent take it by force. For all the prophets and the law prophesied until John came; and if you are willing to accept it, he is Elijah who is to come. Let anyone with ears listen!'

- Jesus began to gather his co-workers from the earliest days of his ministry because he knew he would need other labourers to work alongside him. As the individuals and pairings began to gather around him, it's interesting how often he cited John the Baptist as a key figure and a role model to follow. John had courage and the ability to hold a straight course, never allowing himself to be diverted from what he knew to be right. We could learn something from him.

## Friday 12 December
*Matthew 11:16–19*

Jesus said to the crowds, 'But to what will I compare this generation? It is like children sitting in the market-places and calling to one another,

> "We played the flute for you, and you did not
> dance;
> we wailed, and you did not mourn."

For John came neither eating nor drinking, and they say, "He has a demon"; the Son of Man came eating and drinking, and they say, "Look, a glutton and a drunkard, a friend of tax-collectors and sinners!" Yet wisdom is vindicated by her deeds.'

- Today's Gospel reading takes a bit of working out. Jesus gives us a little insight into how he sometimes must have felt about his own ministry and how it was received. He suggests that those who followed him and those who followed John the Baptist had wildly different experiences, but numbers of them managed to remain stony-faced, whatever was put before them.

## Saturday 13 December
*Matthew 17:10–13*

And the disciples asked him, 'Why, then, do the scribes say that Elijah must come first?' He replied, 'Elijah is indeed coming and will restore all things; but I tell you that Elijah has already come, and they did not recognise him, but they did to him whatever they pleased. So also the Son of Man is about to suffer at their hands.' Then the disciples understood that he was speaking to them about John the Baptist.

- In Jewish tradition, it was thought that the Prophet Elijah would come back to earth before the coming of God's anointed one. His task would be to prepare people for this momentous occasion. The disciples asked Jesus about what was likely to happen, and they did partially pick up that a foreteller in the shape of John the Baptist had been sent but was given as little respect or credence as Elijah himself. One who would prepare the way for the Saviour would be sent, and hints of the Lord's arrival would be given. We find them dotted throughout the Christmas readings and liturgies.

*Something to think and pray about each day this week:*

It is not by chance that we meet John the Baptist and his challenging message during Advent. His call to repent might not excite us, as we're in more of a celebratory mood these weeks, but 'to repent' literally means 'to turn around' or 'to return' (*metanoia*). It does not mean we riddle ourselves with guilt, rather it is an invitation to transformation, to turn away from what is not life-giving for us and embrace that which helps us to live a full, more balanced life. In this way, we create space to welcome Christ's grace and love at Christmas, and we become aware once more of his loving presence in our hearts and in the world around us. This is liberating and enables us to commit to love and the birthing of God in our hearts. How we prepare in these weeks is important and can lead to many blessings. Today John invites the people who have gathered, and us, to a change of heart.

Tríona Doherty and Jane Mellett,
*The Deep End:*
*A Journey with the Gospels in the Year of Matthew*

**The Presence of God**
As I sit here, the beating of my heart,
the ebb and flow of my breathing, the movements of
my mind
are all signs of God's ongoing creation of me.
I pause for a moment and become aware
of this presence of God within me.

**Freedom**
Everything has the potential to draw from me a fuller
love and life. Yet my desires are often fixed, caught,
on illusions of fulfilment. I ask that God, through
my freedom, may orchestrate my desires in a vibrant
loving melody rich in harmony.

**Consciousness**
I ask, how am I within myself today? Am I particularly tired, stressed or off-form? If any of these char-
acteristics apply, can I try to let go of the concerns
that disturb me?

**The Word**
I read the word of God slowly, a few times over, and I listen to what God is saying to me. *(Please turn to the Scripture
on the following pages. Inspiration points are there, should you
need them. When you are ready, return here to continue.)*

**Conversation**

I begin to talk with Jesus about the Scripture I have just read. What part of it strikes a chord in me? Perhaps the words of a friend or a story I have heard recently will slowly rise to the surface of my consciousness. If so, does the story throw light on what the Scripture passage may be trying to say to me?

**Conclusion**

Glory be to the Father, and to the Son, and to the Holy Spirit,
As it was in the beginning, is now and ever shall be,
World without end. Amen.

## Sunday 14 December
## Third Sunday of Advent
*Matthew 11:2–11*

When John heard in prison what the Messiah was doing, he sent word by his disciples and said to him, 'Are you the one who is to come, or are we to wait for another?' Jesus answered them, 'Go and tell John what you hear and see: the blind receive their sight, the lame walk, the lepers are cleansed, the deaf hear, the dead are raised, and the poor have good news brought to them. And blessed is anyone who takes no offence at me.'

As they went away, Jesus began to speak to the crowds about John: 'What did you go out into the wilderness to look at? A reed shaken by the wind? What then did you go out to see? Someone dressed in soft robes? Look, those who wear soft robes are in royal palaces. What then did you go out to see? A prophet? Yes, I tell you, and more than a prophet. This is the one about whom it is written,

"See, I am sending my messenger ahead of you,
    who will prepare your way before you."

Truly I tell you, among those born of women no one has arisen greater than John the Baptist; yet the least in the kingdom of heaven is greater than he.'

- John the Baptist constantly showed himself to be a really reliable companion and precursor to Jesus, but as we see in today's Gospel, even he needed to be reassured at times. Is he having second thoughts? What we were once certain about perhaps now leaves us seeing things in a less black-and-white way.

- When we find our faith wavering, what methods do we have for regaining our confidence in you, Lord?

## Monday 15 December
### Matthew 21:23–27

When he entered the temple, the chief priests and the elders of the people came to him as he was teaching, and said, 'By what authority are you doing these things, and who gave you this authority?' Jesus said to them, 'I will also ask you one question; if you tell me the answer, then I will also tell you by what authority I do these things. Did the baptism of John come from heaven, or was it of human origin?' And they argued with one another, 'If we say, "From heaven", he will say to us, "Why then did you not believe him?" But if we say, "Of human origin", we are afraid of the crowd; for all regard John as a prophet.' So they answered Jesus, 'We do not know.' And he said to them, 'Neither will I tell you by what authority I am doing these things.'

- In the Gospel, Jesus is asked by the religious leaders by whose authority he acts the way he does. Who gave him this authority, they wonder? We already know the answers to these questions because just before this passage we find Jesus driving out the money-lenders and tradesmen from God's house. He acts on his Father's authority. Where in our lives do we allow the sacred to be diminished by day-to-day affairs?

## Tuesday 16 December
*Matthew 21:28–32*

Jesus said to the chief priests and elders, 'What do you think? A man had two sons; he went to the first and said, "Son, go and work in the vineyard today." He answered, "I will not"; but later he changed his mind and went. The father went to the second and said the same; and he answered, "I go, sir"; but he did not go. Which of the two did the will of his father?' They said, 'The first.' Jesus said to them, 'Truly I tell you, the tax-collectors and the prostitutes are going into the kingdom of God ahead of you. For John came to you in the way of righteousness and you did not believe him, but the tax-collectors and the prostitutes believed him; and even after you saw it, you did not change your minds and believe him.'

- Today's Gospel passage reminds us that our actions frequently fail to match our declarations of faith. Jesus could see this often enough in the example of the chief priests and elders who frequently seemed by their words to be saying 'yes' to whatever Jesus was saying, but by their actions indicated that they were clearly intent on doing exactly the opposite. Reflecting on this for a little while might teach us something about our own behaviour.

## Wednesday 17 December
*Matthew 1:1–17*

An account of the genealogy of Jesus the Messiah, the son of David, the son of Abraham.

Abraham was the father of Isaac, and Isaac the father of Jacob, and Jacob the father of Judah and his brothers, and Judah the father of Perez and Zerah by Tamar, and Perez the father of Hezron, and Hezron the father of Aram, and Aram the father of Aminadab, and Aminadab the father of Nahshon, and Nahshon the father of Salmon, and Salmon the father of Boaz by Rahab, and Boaz the father of Obed by Ruth, and Obed the father of Jesse, and Jesse the father of King David.

And David was the father of Solomon by the wife of Uriah, and Solomon the father of Rehoboam, and Rehoboam the father of Abijah, and Abijah the father of Asaph, and Asaph the father of Jehoshaphat, and

Jehoshaphat the father of Joram, and Joram the father of Uzziah, and Uzziah the father of Jotham, and Jotham the father of Ahaz, and Ahaz the father of Hezekiah, and Hezekiah the father of Manasseh, and Manasseh the father of Amos, and Amos the father of Josiah, and Josiah the father of Jechoniah and his brothers, at the time of the deportation to Babylon.

And after the deportation to Babylon: Jechoniah was the father of Salathiel, and Salathiel the father of Zerubbabel, and Zerubbabel the father of Abiud, and Abiud the father of Eliakim, and Eliakim the father of Azor, and Azor the father of Zadok, and Zadok the father of Achim, and Achim the father of Eliud, and Eliud the father of Eleazar, and Eleazar the father of Matthan, and Matthan the father of Jacob, and Jacob the father of Joseph the husband of Mary, of whom Jesus was born, who is called the Messiah.

So all the generations from Abraham to David are fourteen generations; and from David to the deportation to Babylon, fourteen generations; and from the deportation to Babylon to the Messiah, fourteen generations.

- The kind of Gospel passage we have to deal with today gives us, at first sight, very little material we can usefully chew upon. However, it might remind me of the kind of family—and line—I came from myself. It provides a moment to think back on individuals who were huge in the fabric of my own life. Remember, we stand on the shoulders of giants and we pray for those who were so good to us and who generously used their own faith to start us off on our own faith formation.

## Thursday 18 December
*Matthew 1:18–24*

Now the birth of Jesus the Messiah took place in this way. When his mother Mary had been engaged to Joseph, but before they lived together, she was found to be with child from the Holy Spirit. Her husband Joseph, being a righteous man and unwilling to expose her to public disgrace, planned to dismiss her quietly. But just when he had resolved to do this, an angel of the Lord appeared to him in a dream and said, 'Joseph, son of David, do not be afraid to take Mary as your wife, for the child conceived in her is from the Holy Spirit. She will bear a son, and you are to name him Jesus, for he will save his people from their sins.' All this took place to fulfil what had been spoken by the Lord through the prophet:

'Look, the virgin shall conceive and bear a son,
    and they shall name him Emmanuel',

which means, 'God is with us.' When Joseph awoke from sleep, he did as the angel of the Lord commanded him; he took her as his wife.

- Particularly around the Christmas season, numbers of our daily readings give hints of individuals who felt that they were being guided. Often it is not exactly clear how they receive the messages they do. As with Mary herself, or Joseph, or the Wise Men, or the shepherds, or even Simeon or Anna, it doesn't say exactly how the communication was relayed to each individual. It does seem fairly clear, however, that for each of them their own strong faith played a goodly part.

## Friday 19 December
*Luke 1:5–25*

In the days of King Herod of Judea, there was a priest named Zechariah, who belonged to the priestly order of Abijah. His wife was a descendant of Aaron, and her name was Elizabeth. Both of them were righteous before God, living blamelessly according to all the commandments and regulations of the Lord. But they had no children, because Elizabeth was barren, and both were getting on in years.

Once when he was serving as priest before God and his section was on duty, he was chosen by lot, according to the custom of the priesthood, to enter the sanctuary of the Lord and offer incense. Now at the time of the incense-offering, the whole assembly of the people was praying outside. Then there appeared to him an angel of the Lord, standing at the right side of the altar of incense. When Zechariah saw him, he was terrified; and fear overwhelmed him. But the angel said to him, 'Do not be afraid, Zechariah, for your prayer has been heard. Your wife Elizabeth will bear you a son, and you will name him John. You will have joy and gladness, and many will rejoice at his birth, for he will be great in the sight of the Lord. He must never drink wine or strong drink; even before his birth he will be filled with the Holy Spirit. He will turn many of the people of Israel to the Lord their God. With the spirit and power of Elijah he will go before him, to turn the hearts of parents to their children, and the disobedient to the wisdom of the righteous, to make ready a people prepared for the Lord.' Zechariah said to the angel, 'How will I know that this is so? For I am an old man, and my wife is getting on in years.' The angel replied, 'I am Gabriel. I stand in the presence of God, and I have been sent to speak to you and to bring you this good news. But now, because you did not believe my words, which will be fulfilled in their time, you will become mute, unable to speak, until the day these things occur.'

Meanwhile, the people were waiting for Zechariah, and wondered at his delay in the sanctuary. When he did come out, he could not speak to them, and they realised that he had seen a vision in the sanctuary. He kept motioning to them and remained unable to speak. When his time of service was ended, he went to his home.

After those days his wife Elizabeth conceived, and for five months she remained in seclusion. She said, 'This is what the Lord has done for me when he looked favourably on me and took away the disgrace I have endured among my people.'

- Place yourself outside the sanctuary with the other onlookers as Zechariah goes inside the holy place to make his offering. He's probably not expecting anything amazing to happen, but, as the angel Gabriel made clear to him, God had other plans. Zechariah's desire for a child was now going to be fulfilled. The next moments are key. Zechariah doubted that the angel's message would actually become reality. Has my own faith similarly failed me at crucial moments?

## Saturday 20 December
*Luke 1:26–38*

In the sixth month the angel Gabriel was sent by God to a town in Galilee called Nazareth, to a virgin engaged to a man whose name was Joseph, of the house of David. The virgin's name was Mary. And he came to her and said, 'Greetings, favoured one! The Lord is with you.' But she was much perplexed by his words and pondered what sort of greeting this might be. The angel said to her, 'Do not be afraid, Mary, for you have found favour with God. And now, you will conceive in your womb and bear a son, and you will name him Jesus. He will be great, and will be called the Son of the Most High, and the Lord God will give to him the throne of his ancestor David. He will reign over the house of Jacob for ever, and of his kingdom there will be no end.' Mary said to the angel, 'How can this be, since I am a virgin?' The angel said to her, 'The Holy Spirit will come upon you, and the power of the Most High will overshadow you; therefore the child to be born will be holy; he will be called Son of God. And now, your relative Elizabeth in her old age has also conceived a son; and this is the sixth month for her who was said to be barren. For nothing will be impossible with God.' Then Mary said, 'Here am I, the servant of the Lord; let it be with me according to your word.' Then the angel departed from her.

- Yesterday, we found ourselves with Zechariah and noticed how his doubt and skepticism almost threw a spanner in the works. In today's scene, Our Lady reacts in an altogether different manner. Even though she has no clear picture of what God is asking her to do, or what the implications of those actions might mean for her, her general orientation is to say 'yes' to whatever is being offered by God. Her generosity of spirit facilitates God's arrangements rather than obstructing them.

## Fourth Week of Advent
# 21–27 December 2025

*Something to think and pray about each day this week:*

In religious terms we would call Joseph a faithful type of guy, observant in religious thought and practice. The visit from the angel tests his faithfulness to God and to Mary. He doesn't let them down. He was called to be the carer of Jesus and Mary and to find a new openness to the mystery of God.

A temptation of religion is to tie things down too much. Good religion is open to the mystery of life, however life challenges us and calls us.

True religion is open to mystery. We need a church lit with the light of God, as Joseph was. His burden was lifted when he was open to God, to taking Mary home as his wife, no matter what others might think.

This is the annunciation to Joseph—the word of God from the angel to Joseph in a dream. It opened him to a huge new meaning in life. We accept this word as a central part of our lives, and the next time we meet the word, it will be made flesh.

Donal Neary SJ,
*Gospel Reflections for Sundays of Year A*

### The Presence of God

Dear Jesus, I come to you today longing for your presence. I desire to love you as you love me. May nothing ever separate me from you.

### Freedom

Lord, grant me the grace to be free from the excesses of this life. Let me not get caught up with the desire for wealth. Keep my heart and mind free to love and serve you.

### Consciousness

Where do I sense hope, encouragement and growth in my life? By looking back over the past few months, I may be able to see which activities and occasions have produced rich fruit. If I do notice such areas, I will determine to give those areas both time and space in the future.

### The Word

God speaks to each of us individually. I listen attentively to hear what he is saying to me. Read the text a few times, then listen. *(Please turn to the Scripture on the following pages. Inspiration points are there, should you need them. When you are ready, return here to continue.)*

**Conversation**
What is stirring in me as I pray? Am I consoled, troubled, left cold? I imagine Jesus standing or sitting at my side, and I share my feelings with him.

**Conclusion**
Glory be to the Father, and to the Son, and to the Holy Spirit,
As it was in the beginning, is now and ever shall be,
World without end. Amen.

## Sunday 21 December
## Fourth Sunday of Advent
*Matthew 1:18–24*

Now the birth of Jesus the Messiah took place in this way. When his mother Mary had been engaged to Joseph, but before they lived together, she was found to be with child from the Holy Spirit. Her husband Joseph, being a righteous man and unwilling to expose her to public disgrace, planned to dismiss her quietly. But just when he had resolved to do this, an angel of the Lord appeared to him in a dream and said, 'Joseph, son of David, do not be afraid to take Mary as your wife, for the child conceived in her is from the Holy Spirit. She will bear a son, and you are to name him Jesus, for he will save his people from their sins.' All this took place to fulfil what had been spoken by the Lord through the prophet:

'Look, the virgin shall conceive and bear a son,
    and they shall name him Emmanuel',

which means, 'God is with us.' When Joseph awoke from sleep, he did as the angel of the Lord commanded him; he took her as his wife.

- The Gospel passages we are given around the Christmas season are in many ways unlike anything we are given during the rest of the liturgical year. They have a sort of mystical, somewhat dreamlike quality, and it's not unusual to find one or two of the characters receiving visits, wisdom, or information from figures who are clearly something other than human. Angels feature prominently, as do dreams, and great faith and trust are required on the part of those on the receiving end. Notice Joseph particularly in this regard. It's very inspiring to see how some of those visited respond with such openness.

## Monday 22 December
*Luke 1:46–56*

And Mary said,
>   'My soul magnifies the Lord, ❀
>> and my spirit rejoices in God my Saviour,
> for he has looked with favour on the lowliness
>> of his servant.
>> Surely, from now on all generations will call
>> me blessed;
> for the Mighty One has done great things
>> for me,
>> and holy is his name.
> His mercy is for those who fear him
>> from generation to generation.
> He has shown strength with his arm;
>> he has scattered the proud in the thoughts
>> of their hearts.

He has brought down the powerful from their
thrones,
and lifted up the lowly;
he has filled the hungry with good things,
and sent the rich away empty.
He has helped his servant Israel,
in remembrance of his mercy,
according to the promise he made to our
ancestors,
to Abraham and to his descendants for
ever.'

And Mary remained with her for about three months
and then returned to her home.

- St Ignatius mentions regularly in his *Spiritual Exercises* that he found it very beneficial to go first to Our Lady and ask her to act as his intercessor regarding whatever favour he was asking for during his times of prayer. Mary does not appear too often in the Bible, but whenever she does, it is usually with very telling effect. Sometimes, as at the marriage feast at Cana, her input and activity do not appear too critical. It's only on a second or third reading that you sometimes notice that her relationship with her son, and the timing and wisdom of her intervention, affect the outcome tremendously.

# Tuesday 23 December

*Luke 1:57–66*

Now the time came for Elizabeth to give birth, and she bore a son. Her neighbours and relatives heard that the Lord had shown his great mercy to her, and they rejoiced with her.

On the eighth day they came to circumcise the child, and they were going to name him Zechariah after his father. But his mother said, 'No; he is to be called John.' They said to her, 'None of your relatives has this name.' Then they began motioning to his father to find out what name he wanted to give him. He asked for a writing-tablet and wrote, 'His name is John.' And all of them were amazed. Immediately his mouth was opened and his tongue freed, and he began to speak, praising God. Fear came over all their neighbours, and all these things were talked about throughout the entire hill country of Judea. All who heard them pondered them and said, 'What then will this child become?' For, indeed, the hand of the Lord was with him.

- We came upon Zechariah some days ago, and this time he shows himself in a very different light. He had initially been very unsure of how he should act when the angel Gabriel predicted his future. Gabriel's prophecy seemed so unlikely to occur that Zechariah was loath to take much notice of it, but the penalty for his disbelief—being struck dumb—changed his tune. This time, when asked what the name of the newborn baby should be, he asked for a tablet and wrote, 'His name is John.' Not only had his tongue been loosened but his heart had been made more receptive as well.

## Wednesday 24 December
*Luke 1:67–79*

Then his father Zechariah was filled with the Holy Spirit and spoke this prophecy:

'Blessed be the Lord God of Israel,
> for he has looked favourably on his people
> > and redeemed them.
He has raised up a mighty saviour for us
> in the house of his servant David,
as he spoke through the mouth of his holy
> prophets from of old,
> > that we would be saved from our enemies
> > and from the hand of
> > all who hate us.
Thus he has shown the mercy promised to our
> ancestors,
> and has remembered his holy covenant,
the oath that he swore to our ancestor Abraham,
> to grant us that we, being rescued from the
> > hands of our enemies,

might serve him without fear, in holiness and
    righteousness
    before him all our days.
And you, child, will be called the prophet of the
    Most High;
    for you will go before the Lord to prepare
        his ways,
to give knowledge of salvation to his people
    by the forgiveness of their sins.
By the tender mercy of our God,
    the dawn from on high will break upon us,
to give light to those who sit in darkness and in
    the shadow of death,
    to guide our feet into the way of peace.'

- Zechariah, father of John the Baptist, who had nothing to say since the annunciation of John's birth, breaks his silence with a vengeance. He makes use of the gift he has been given by the Holy Spirit and produces a great hymn of praise. He appreciates the wonderful works that have come about—things he never expected—and wants to make sure that his appreciation does not go unnoticed. We can take the time to spend some moments in wonder at the gifts given to us during this season—and make our gratitude known—first to ourselves and then to those who should be communicated with.

# Thursday 25 December
# The Nativity of the Lord

*John 1:1–18*

In the beginning was the Word, and the Word was with God, and the Word was God. He was in the beginning with God. All things came into being through him, and without him not one thing came into being. What has come into being in him was life, and the life was the light of all people. The light shines in the darkness, and the darkness did not overcome it.

There was a man sent from God, whose name was John. He came as a witness to testify to the light, so that all might believe through him. He himself was not the light, but he came to testify to the light. The true light, which enlightens everyone, was coming into the world.

He was in the world, and the world came into being through him; yet the world did not know him. He came to what was his own, and his own people did not accept him. But to all who received him, who believed in his name, he gave power to become children of God, who were born, not of blood or of the will of the flesh or of the will of man, but of God.

And the Word became flesh and lived among us, and we have seen his glory, the glory as of a father's only son, full of grace and truth. (John testified to him and cried out, 'This was he of whom I said,

"He who comes after me ranks ahead of me because he was before me."') From his fullness we have all received, grace upon grace. The law indeed was given through Moses; grace and truth came through Jesus Christ. No one has ever seen God. It is God the only Son, who is close to the Father's heart, who has made him known.

- John's Gospel account begins in heaven. It quickly brings us back down to earth when we're told that the Word was made flesh, and lived amongst us. All God wanted to say to us he said through his Son, who consistently told us that God wishes to pour out his goodness upon us. He sent his Son for this very purpose—that we may have life and have it to the full.

## Friday 26 December
## St Stephen
### Matthew 10:17–22

Jesus said to his disciples, 'Beware of them, for they will hand you over to councils and flog you in their synagogues; and you will be dragged before governors and kings because of me, as a testimony to them and the Gentiles. When they hand you over, do not worry about how you are to speak or what you are to say; for what you are to say will be given to you at that time; for it is not you who speak, but the Spirit of your Father speaking through you. Brother will betray brother to death, and a father his child, and children will rise against parents and have them put to death; and you will be hated by all because of my name. But the one who endures to the end will be saved.'

- Today, we look towards the figure of St Stephen, one of the pillars of the early church, and we reflect upon the devastating effect his violent death must have had upon the early Christian community. How dark the times must have seemed to them . . . was this the end of their existence as a group of early Christian followers? It must have seemed so. In reality, their despair sowed the seeds of fresh growth for them. It was from amongst the group of individuals who had so cruelly murdered Stephen that the towering figure of St Paul emerged, a tiny light springing from the darkness and desolation.

## Saturday 27 December
## St John, Apostle and Evangelist
*John 20:2–8*

So she ran and went to Simon Peter and the other disciple, the one whom Jesus loved, and said to them, 'They have taken the Lord out of the tomb, and we do not know where they have laid him.' Then Peter and the other disciple set out and went towards the tomb. The two were running together, but the other disciple outran Peter and reached the tomb first. He bent down to look in and saw the linen wrappings lying there, but he did not go in. Then Simon Peter came, following him, and went into the tomb. He saw the linen wrappings lying there, and the cloth that had been on Jesus' head, not lying with the linen wrappings but rolled up in a place by itself. Then the other disciple, who reached the tomb first, also went in, and he saw and believed.

- On this, the feast of John the Evangelist, we might take time out to think of and pray for people who come into our lives and have the power or gift of bringing us rays of sunshine and hope when moments of surrounding gloom may threaten to engulf us. In art, we often see John portrayed as a younger figure, sticking close to Peter when the elder man needs some shaft of energy or enthusiasm to keep him from falling or drowning. You can almost see the two racing towards the tomb after they have spoken to Mary Magdalene. We imagine a gentle breeze blowing on the gray embers surrounding their hearts as they hurry along.

# 28 December 2025–3 January 2026

*Something to think and pray about each day this week:*

As we celebrate Christmas, we are asked to open up our hearts, to make our hearts a crib, a place to welcome and encounter Jesus. What does this mean? As we hear the Christmas story today, what effect does it have on us?

Perhaps we are like the shepherds, bubbling over with joy.

We might identify with Mary, still trying to figure out what it all means. There is room for both.

There is a depth and intimacy to Mary's understanding of Jesus, whereas the shepherds have perhaps only scratched the surface. Our faith and our relationship with God go through seasons. The ups and downs of life can take us by surprise, and we might find ourselves looking at things in a different way. When the flurry of Advent is over, Christmas has a way of stopping us in our tracks, giving us time to rest in wonderment and give thanks for God's faithfulness in our lives. This is a time to sit with Mary as she treasures and ponders.

Tríona Doherty and Jane Mellett,
*The Deep End:*
*A Journey with the Gospels in the Year of Matthew*

### The Presence of God

'I am standing at the door, knocking,' says the Lord. What a wonderful privilege that the Lord of all creation desires to come to me. I welcome his presence.

### Freedom

I will ask God's help to be free from my own preoccupations, to be open to God in this time of prayer, to come to know, love, and serve God more.

### Consciousness

In God's loving presence I unwind the past day, starting from now and looking back, moment by moment. I gather in all the goodness and light, in gratitude. I attend to the shadows and what they say to me, seeking healing, courage, forgiveness.

### The Word

Now I turn to the Scripture set out for me this day. I read slowly over the words and see if any sentence or sentiment appeals to me. *(Please turn to the Scripture on the following pages. Inspiration points are there, should you need them. When you are ready, return here to continue.)*

### Conversation

Sometimes I wonder what I might say if I were to meet you in person, Lord.

I think I might say, 'Thank you', because you are always there for me.

**Conclusion**
I thank God for these moments we have spent together and for any insights I have been given concerning the text.

# Sunday 28 December
# The Holy Family
*Matthew 2:13–15, 19–23*

Now after they had left, an angel of the Lord appeared to Joseph in a dream and said, 'Get up, take the child and his mother, and flee to Egypt, and remain there until I tell you; for Herod is about to search for the child, to destroy him.' Then Joseph got up, took the child and his mother by night, and went to Egypt, and remained there until the death of Herod. This was to fulfil what had been spoken by the Lord through the prophet, 'Out of Egypt I have called my son.' . . .

When Herod died, an angel of the Lord suddenly appeared in a dream to Joseph in Egypt and said, 'Get up, take the child and his mother, and go to the land of Israel, for those who were seeking the child's life are dead.' Then Joseph got up, took the child and his mother, and went to the land of Israel. But when he heard that Archelaus was ruling over Judea in place of his father Herod, he was afraid to go there. And after being warned in a dream, he went away to the district of Galilee. There he made his home in a town called Nazareth, so that what had been spoken through the prophets might be fulfilled, 'He will be called a Nazorean.'

- Almost nothing has gone as the Holy Family might have expected. First, having to uproot themselves from Bethlehem, they find themselves forced to travel to Egypt to escape the murderous tactics of King Herod, and even after his death it seemed safest to travel northwards to the little village of Nazareth. We can visualise their plight and are reminded of it by the many migrants who find themselves in equally hazardous conditions today, with nowhere safe to lay their heads, and in need of the support, care, and guidance of those around them to stay afloat.

## Monday 29 December
*Luke 2:22–35*

When the time came for their purification according to the law of Moses, they brought him up to Jerusalem to present him to the Lord (as it is written in the law of the Lord, 'Every firstborn male shall be designated as holy to the Lord'), and they offered a sacrifice according to what is stated in the law of the Lord, 'a pair of turtle-doves or two young pigeons.'

Now there was a man in Jerusalem whose name was Simeon; this man was righteous and devout, looking forward to the consolation of Israel, and the Holy Spirit rested on him. It had been revealed to him by the Holy Spirit that he would not see death before he had seen the Lord's Messiah. Guided by the Spirit, Simeon came into the temple; and when the parents brought in the child Jesus, to do for him what was customary under the law, Simeon took him in his arms and praised God, saying,

> 'Master, now you are dismissing your servant
>    in peace,
>       according to your word;
> for my eyes have seen your salvation,
>    which you have prepared in the presence of
>       all peoples,
> a light for revelation to the Gentiles
>    and for glory to your people Israel.'

And the child's father and mother were amazed at what was being said about him. Then Simeon blessed them and said to his mother Mary, 'This child is destined for the falling and the rising of many in Israel, and to be a sign that will be opposed so that the inner thoughts of many will be revealed—and a sword will pierce your own soul too.'

- New characters keep appearing in our Christmas story and prayer. Today we have Simeon, who believes a promise that he will not die before he first lays eyes on the Christ-child. He makes his way to the temple each day and sits down patiently to wait. And then, one day, when hope has almost gone, he spots a woman coming down the dusty road, seated on a donkey with an infant in her arms, the little party led by Joseph. Simeon rushes over and somehow recognises that this is the moment he so longed for. How did he know? How did he have the faith to keep on believing? We are not told. We have to work it out for ourselves.

## Tuesday 30 December
*Luke 2:36–40*

There was also a prophet, Anna the daughter of Phanuel, of the tribe of Asher. She was of a great age, having lived with her husband for seven years after her marriage, then as a widow to the age of eighty-four. She never left the temple but worshipped there with fasting and prayer night and day. At that moment she came, and began to praise God and to speak about the child to all who were looking for the redemption of Jerusalem.

When they had finished everything required by the law of the Lord, they returned to Galilee, to their own town of Nazareth. The child grew and became strong, filled with wisdom; and the favour of God was upon him.

• Anna appears only once in the Christmas story, but she has some notable qualities. She is no longer young, but her faith and hope have not been dimmed by age. She, like Simeon, knows where to come and is rewarded for her diligence. Her great constancy leads her to the temple, and her fasting and prayer are rewarded. We pray today for some of Anna's constancy and ask that our own efforts may be rewarded by a sense, Lord, of your presence, to keep us moving onwards towards you.

## Wednesday 31 December
*John 1:1–18*

In the beginning was the Word, and the Word was with God, and the Word was God. He was in the beginning with God. All things came into being through him, and without him not one thing came into being. What has come into being in him was life, and the life was the light of all people. The light shines in the darkness, and the darkness did not overcome it.

There was a man sent from God, whose name was John. He came as a witness to testify to the light, so that all might believe through him. He himself was not the light, but he came to testify to the light. The true light, which enlightens everyone, was coming into the world.

He was in the world, and the world came into being through him; yet the world did not know him. He came to what was his own, and his own people did not accept him. But to all who received him, who believed in his name, he gave power to become children of God, who were born, not of blood or of the will of the flesh or of the will of man, but of God.

And the Word became flesh and lived among us, and we have seen his glory, the glory as of a father's only son, full of grace and truth. (John testified to him and cried out, 'This was he of whom I said, "He who comes after me ranks ahead of me because he was before me."') From his fullness we have all received, grace upon grace. The law indeed was given through Moses; grace and truth came through Jesus Christ. No one has ever seen God. It is God the only Son, who is close to the Father's heart, who has made him known.

- This is the 'Christmas gospel'. Christmas is not simply the celebration of the birth of the baby Jesus, but the awesome mystery of the Incarnation of God. God pitched his tent among us and remains among us as a human being for ever.

- The world did not know him. His own people, the leaders of the Jews, did not accept him. We have accepted him, and our vocation is to make his light shine for the whole world.

## Thursday 1 January
## Mary, the Holy Mother of God
*Luke 2:16–21*

So they went with haste and found Mary and Joseph, and the child lying in the manger. When they saw this, they made known what had been told them about this child; and all who heard it were amazed at what the shepherds told them. But Mary treasured all these words and pondered them in her heart. The shepherds returned, glorifying and praising God for all they had heard and seen, as it had been told them.

After eight days had passed, it was time to circumcise the child; and he was called Jesus, the name given by the angel before he was conceived in the womb.

• Today the shepherds make their presence known to us. They are simple folk, well used to the mountains, and know how to look after themselves as well as their sheep. Somehow their very simplicity of life seems to have helped them to be like an open book before God. They find where he rests and feel at ease with his parents, simple folk like themselves. Mary listens to whatever they have to say and ponders what she hears over quite a long period. We try to imitate their example.

# Friday 2 January
*John 1:19–28*

This is the testimony given by John when the Jews sent priests and Levites from Jerusalem to ask him, 'Who are you?' He confessed and did not deny it, but confessed, 'I am not the Messiah.' And they asked him, 'What then? Are you Elijah?' He said, 'I am not.' 'Are you the prophet?' He answered, 'No.' Then they said to him, 'Who are you? Let us have an answer for those who sent us. What do you say about yourself?' He said,

> 'I am the voice of one crying out in the
>      wilderness,
> "Make straight the way of the Lord"',

as the prophet Isaiah said.

Now they had been sent from the Pharisees. They asked him, 'Why then are you baptising if you are neither the Messiah, nor Elijah, nor the prophet?' John answered them, 'I baptise with water. Among you stands one whom you do not know, the one who is coming after me; I am not worthy to untie the thong of his sandal.' This took place in Bethany across the Jordan where John was baptising.

- On most of the occasions when we meet John the Baptist in the Gospel stories, we tend to be struck by how forthright and consistent he is. Even in the way he answers the questions put to him by the Jews in today's passage we can see that he does not cloud the issue. They ask, 'Who are you and what's your business?' He tells them straight out, 'I'm not the one you should be surveying but I'm here to prepare a way for the saviour.' John points towards Jesus and the path he is laying out. For those prepared to listen it is as clear a signpost as one could wish for.

## Saturday 3 January
### John 1:29–34

The next day he saw Jesus coming towards him and declared, 'Here is the Lamb of God who takes away the sin of the world! This is he of whom I said, "After me comes a man who ranks ahead of me because he was before me." I myself did not know him; but I came baptising with water for this reason, that he might be revealed to Israel.' And John testified, 'I saw the Spirit descending from heaven like a dove, and it remained on him. I myself did not know him, but the one who sent me to baptise with water said to me, "He on whom you see the Spirit descend and remain is the one who baptises with the Holy Spirit." And I myself have seen and have testified that this is the Son of God.'

- As we read today's Gospel we are given the example of John the Baptist as a person of great faith, but also one who is more than prepared to move his followers on to a teacher who is altogether greater than himself. Jesus wants to talk with us directly, but he sometimes makes use of special figures who can open a door to him. John is one of these, as were Andrew and Peter. Spend a little time reminding yourself of people who were guides for you as they generously tried to help you develop your own faith.

*Something to think and pray about each day this week:*

The Wise Men were probably astronomers and philosophers from the region of Persia, but most importantly of all they were seekers. They looked to the skies for astronomical signs which would foretell the birth of a powerful leader. They were awake to the signs of the times. We don't know details of their religious affiliations and it really does not matter, for this story of the Wise Men is the story of people of all cultures, all countries, and all faiths who make a journey in search of God.

The arrival of the Wise Men in Bethlehem is a moment of great joy and grace, as, 'on entering the house, they saw the child with Mary his mother; and they knelt down and paid him homage'. God is found in the simple spaces. Let us have the courage to take the risk and move out of our comfort zones in search of Jesus, just as the Wise Men did. They had no idea of what awaited them, but the Gospel speaks of their delight and joy when they arrived at that place.

Tríona Doherty and Jane Mellett,
*The Deep End:*
*A Journey with the Gospels in the Year of Luke*

## The Presence of God

At any time of the day or night we can call on Jesus. He is always waiting, listening for our call. What a wonderful blessing.

No phone needed, no e-mails, just a whisper.

## Freedom

If God were trying to tell me something, would I know? If God were reassuring me or challenging me, would I notice? I ask for the grace to be free of my own preoccupations and open to what God may be saying to me.

## Consciousness

Help me, Lord, become more conscious of your presence. Teach me to recognise your presence in others. Fill my heart with gratitude for the times your love has been shown to me through the care of others.

## The Word

In this expectant state of mind, please turn to the text for the day with confidence. Believe that the Holy Spirit is present and may reveal whatever the passage has to say to you. Read reflectively, listening with a third ear to what may be going on in your heart. *(Please turn to the Scripture on the following pages. Inspiration points are there, should you need them. When you are ready, return here to continue.)*

**Conversation**
Conversation requires talking and listening. As I talk to Jesus, may I also learn to pause and listen. I picture the gentleness in his eyes and the love in his smile. I can be totally honest with Jesus as I tell him my worries and cares. I will open my heart to Jesus as I tell him my fears and doubts. I will ask him to help me place myself fully in his care, knowing that he always desires good for me.

**Conclusion**
I thank God for these moments we have spent together and for any insights I have been given concerning the text.

# Sunday 4 January
# Second Sunday of Christmas/
# The Epiphany of the Lord (USA)

*John 1:1–5, 9–14*

In the beginning was the Word, and the Word was with God, and the Word was God. He was in the beginning with God. All things came into being through him, and without him not one thing came into being. What has come into being in him was life, and the life was the light of all people. The light shines in the darkness, and the darkness did not overcome it. . . . The true light, which enlightens everyone, was coming into the world.

He was in the world, and the world came into being through him; yet the world did not know him. He came to what was his own, and his own people did not accept him. But to all who received him, who believed in his name, he gave power to become children of God, who were born, not of blood or of the will of the flesh or of the will of man, but of God.

And the Word became flesh and lived among us, and we have seen his glory, the glory as of a father's only son, full of grace and truth.

- Every year has moments of light and shade, so this is an opportunity to recall the good times and good things that came our way during the past year with gratitude and thanks, whilst not forgetting the moments that were much more challenging. We try to remember that wherever our lives take us—even in the less desirable situations we may have to face—God walks with us on the journey.

## Monday 5 January
*John 1:43–51*

The next day Jesus decided to go to Galilee. He found Philip and said to him, 'Follow me.' Now Philip was from Bethsaida, the city of Andrew and Peter. Philip found Nathanael and said to him, 'We have found him about whom Moses in the law and also the prophets wrote, Jesus son of Joseph from Nazareth.' Nathanael said to him, 'Can anything good come out of Nazareth?' Philip said to him, 'Come and see.' When Jesus saw Nathanael coming towards him, he said of him, 'Here is truly an Israelite in whom there is no deceit!' Nathanael asked him, 'Where did you come to know me?' Jesus answered, 'I saw you under the fig tree before Philip called you.' Nathanael replied, 'Rabbi, you are the Son of God! You are the King of Israel!' Jesus answered, 'Do you believe because I told you that I saw you under the fig tree? You will see greater things than these.' And he said to him, 'Very truly, I tell you, you will see heaven opened and the angels of God ascending and descending upon the Son of Man.'

- Philip has one particular talent, which brought joy and spiritual nourishment to many. He seemed to have the gift of being able to hang around the periphery of visitors who came seeking Christ's company but who were shyer than they might have liked to be and were reluctant to introduce themselves to the Lord or to ask Jesus for whatever it was they required. If I similarly find it hard to intercede with Christ on my own or others' behalf, perhaps Philip might take on for me the task that I find so difficult.

## Tuesday 6 January
## The Epiphany of the Lord (Ireland)
*Matthew 2:1–6*

In the time of King Herod, after Jesus was born in Bethlehem of Judea, wise men from the East came to Jerusalem, asking, 'Where is the child who has been born king of the Jews? For we observed his star at its rising, and have come to pay him homage.' When King Herod heard this, he was frightened, and all Jerusalem with him; and calling together all the chief priests and scribes of the people, he inquired of them where the Messiah was to be born. They told him, 'In Bethlehem of Judea; for so it has been written by the prophet:

"And you, Bethlehem, in the land of Judah,
are by no means least among the rulers of
Judah;
for from you shall come a ruler
who is to shepherd my people Israel."'

- In 'Journey of the Magi', T. S. Eliot asks us to imagine the Wise Men from the East as they notice something above them in the skies that they did not understand. Their skill and interest was to interpret the events they saw going on around them on earth, and this talent meant that they were prepared to go to quite a lot of trouble to try and find out what the strange star they had noticed might mean. Could it indicate that a new king had been born to the Jews?

## Wednesday 7 January
*Matthew 4:12–17, 23–25*

Now when Jesus heard that John had been arrested, he withdrew to Galilee. He left Nazareth and made his home in Capernaum by the lake, in the territory of Zebulun and Naphtali, so that what had been spoken through the prophet Isaiah might be fulfilled:

'Land of Zebulun, land of Naphtali,
on the road by the sea, across the Jordan,
Galilee of the Gentiles—

the people who sat in darkness
    have seen a great light,
and for those who sat in the region and shadow
    of death
    light has dawned.'

From that time Jesus began to proclaim, 'Repent, for the kingdom of heaven has come near.' . . .

Jesus went throughout Galilee, teaching in their synagogues and proclaiming the good news of the kingdom and curing every disease and every sickness among the people. So his fame spread throughout all Syria, and they brought to him all the sick, those who were afflicted with various diseases and pains, demoniacs, epileptics, and paralytics, and he cured them. And great crowds followed him from Galilee, the Decapolis, Jerusalem, Judea, and from beyond the Jordan.

• It had been foretold that the people who lived in darkness would see a great light, and Jesus was now going to spell out in clear detail what this light would consist of. As the work of Jesus begins to grow, we notice something stirring within the onlookers who hang on his every word. Grey embers of faith are beginning to feel a gentle breeze blowing in their direction. Almost without their knowing it, a spark of hope is being reignited. Ask that the spark of anticipation may also be given to you.

## Thursday 8 January
*Mark 6:34–44*

As he went ashore, he saw a great crowd; and he had compassion for them, because they were like sheep without a shepherd; and he began to teach them many things. When it grew late, his disciples came to him and said, 'This is a deserted place, and the hour is now very late; send them away so that they may go into the surrounding country and villages and buy something for themselves to eat.' But he answered them, 'You give them something to eat.' They said to him, 'Are we to go and buy two hundred denarii worth of bread, and give it to them to eat?' And he said to them, 'How many loaves have you? Go and see.' When they had found out, they said, 'Five, and two fish.' Then he ordered them to get all the people to sit down in groups on the green grass. So they sat down in groups of hundreds and of fifties. Taking the five loaves and the two fish, he looked up to heaven, and blessed and broke the loaves, and gave them to his disciples to set before the people; and he divided the two fish among them all. And all ate and were filled; and they took up twelve baskets full of broken pieces and of the fish. Those who had eaten the loaves numbered five thousand men.

- Those who come to listen to the Lord, even without knowing it themselves, probably sense that they need both their bodies and their spirits to be re-energised. Does he not try to do exactly that for us? He not only wants to feed our various hungers but can use whatever talents we might have to make good the hungers of those whom we may find ourselves encountering. Think of the times you have been able to be a person for others. Ask that those sort of occasions might present themselves again and that Jesus may strengthen you to be a positive provider for those around you.

## Friday 9 January
### Mark 6:45–52

Immediately he made his disciples get into the boat and go on ahead to the other side, to Bethsaida, while he dismissed the crowd. After saying farewell to them, he went up on the mountain to pray.

When evening came, the boat was out on the lake, and he was alone on the land. When he saw that they were straining at the oars against an adverse wind, he came towards them early in the morning, walking on the lake. He intended to pass them by. But when they saw him walking on the lake, they thought it was a ghost and cried out; for they all saw him and were terrified. But immediately he spoke to them and said,

'Take heart, it is I; do not be afraid.' Then he got into the boat with them and the wind ceased. And they were utterly astounded, for they did not understand about the loaves, but their hearts were hardened.

- It's pretty clear, Lord, that concern for your disciples was never too far from your mind. When you saw them once again getting themselves into a troublesome situation, you acted. I ask that when I find myself in tight corners and fairly terrified, you will—as you did with your disciples here—likewise come to my aid with the same words, 'Take heart, it is I; do not be afraid.'

## Saturday 10 January
### Luke 4:14–22

Then Jesus, filled with the power of the Spirit, returned to Galilee, and a report about him spread through all the surrounding country. He began to teach in their synagogues and was praised by everyone.

When he came to Nazareth, where he had been brought up, he went to the synagogue on the sabbath day, as was his custom. He stood up to read, and the scroll of the prophet Isaiah was given to him. He unrolled the scroll and found the place where it was written:

'The Spirit of the Lord is upon me,
     because he has anointed me
          to bring good news to the poor.
He has sent me to proclaim release to the
     captives
          and recovery of sight to the blind,
               to let the oppressed go free,
     to proclaim the year of the Lord's favour.'

And he rolled up the scroll, gave it back to the attendant, and sat down. The eyes of all in the synagogue were fixed on him. Then he began to say to them, 'Today this scripture has been fulfilled in your hearing.' All spoke well of him and were amazed at the gracious words that came from his mouth. They said, 'Is not this Joseph's son?'

- We have a Zoom prayer group in our parish and recently, most unusually, every member of the group except for one had chosen 'Today this scripture has been fulfilled in your hearing.' I think that you spoke very directly to those before you. Many of us feel you are speaking these words directly to us as well: 'He has anointed me to bring good news . . . [and] to proclaim release to the captives". Are these the very words you want me to hear also, Lord?

# An Advent Retreat

This short retreat invites you to reflect on a handful of readings that have particular resonance during the season of Advent. Before engaging with each session of the retreat, you are invited to step back from the world, take time out from the busyness and noise of everyday life, by reading the Reflection for Advent on p. 78. At the beginning of each session you will be guided through a short stillness exercise, which will help you to slow your breathing and immerse yourself in the scripture readings and reflections.

Each of the four sessions presents two readings, one from the Old Testament and one from the New Testament, each followed by a short reflection. When you have reflected on the readings, you may want to 'talk to God' about anything that has arisen for you during your reflection. There are prompts for this conversation at the end of each session, should you need them.

If you haven't made a retreat like this before, one question to consider is how long you feel that you can devote to each session of the retreat. It's good to decide this in advance and try to stick to it. Don't give up too soon if the prayer seems a little dull or continue too long if it seems to be going well. Each of the retreat sessions should last about twenty minutes. Just choose a time that you can comfortably fit into your routine, having spent a few minutes preparing yourself and perhaps some more time afterwards noting in writing, in pictures or in whatever way you choose what the key points of invitation or resistance were for you. Whatever your responses and reactions, keep a brief note, as a pattern may emerge that proves a helpful guide when you look back.

You might also like to give some thought to what time of day is best for you to pray—morning, evening, or in the middle of the day? This might also suggest another question: Where will you find it easiest to pray and reflect in this way?

Finally, ask yourself why you are making this retreat. What are the gifts and graces you would hope to receive from God during these times of prayer? Make sure that you start the prayer by asking God for these gifts and graces and try to be open to whatever else God wants to give you. Often we do not know what we really need!

When you have taken a while to consider these questions, you'll be ready to begin this prayerful time of reflecting on 'stepping beyond'. Before you start, take a moment to become aware of God's welcoming gaze of love on you as you meet him in this way. Become aware also of all those others around the world who are praying this retreat alongside you and know that you are part of this worldwide community of prayer.

## A Reflection for Advent

Advent is waiting for the birth of Jesus,
but it's a strange waiting:
we are waiting each year for someone we know
    is here!

   We recall in Advent
that the Lord Jesus has come among us,
is present all the time
and will come again in glory.

   He is the child who is born each year,
for the world always needs its God and Saviour.
He is the child awaited each year,
for our lives are new each year,
and we need him in different ways at different
    stages of life,
and the world has different needs of God at
    different times.

   We need the child of peace to be born
in our wars and violence,
the child of wisdom in our search for truth and
    meaning,
the child of gentleness in a world that can be
    harsh and greedy.

We need to know in Jesus
that birth and life
are among the most precious gifts of God,
and that in the birth of Jesus each year
is the everlasting promise of God
to be with us.

And Advent looks ahead,
letting us see that the life of Jesus is never over,
that the truth of Jesus is always spoken,
that the love of Jesus is always real,
and that he will one day be seen in glory.

For we are people of Advent and Easter,
of waiting and of resurrection;
we are people of earth and heaven,
as he is the son of God and son of Mary,
and leads us through our life on earth
to the eternal glory of heaven.

## Session 1

### Invitation to Stillness

We usually prepare for an important meeting or conversation by focusing our mind and body so that we can be fully present. We begin today by inviting you to notice your breathing, the rhythm of it, and the feel and sound of each breath as you inhale and exhale. With each in-breath, allow yourself to focus on the here and now. With each out-breath, let go of any tension or concern you may feel other than being here, still, in this space.

### Reading

*Isaiah 29:17–24*

> Shall not Lebanon in a very little while
> > become a fruitful field,
> > and the fruitful field be regarded as a forest?
> On that day the deaf shall hear
> > the words of a scroll,
> and out of their gloom and darkness
> > the eyes of the blind shall see.
> The meek shall obtain fresh joy in the Lord,
> > and the neediest people shall exult in the
> > > Holy One of Israel.
> For the tyrant shall be no more,
> > and the scoffer shall cease to be;
> > all those alert to do evil shall be cut off—

those who cause a person to lose a lawsuit,
who set a trap for the arbiter in the gate,
   and without grounds deny justice to the one
    in the right.
Therefore thus says the LORD, who redeemed
  Abraham, concerning the house of Jacob:
No longer shall Jacob be ashamed,
   no longer shall his face grow pale.
For when he sees his children,
   the work of my hands, in his midst,
   they will sanctify my name;
they will sanctify the Holy One of Jacob,
   and will stand in awe of the God of Israel.
And those who err in spirit will come to
  understanding,
   and those who grumble will accept
    instruction.

## Reflect

All of us have something in mind that we really anticipate for Christmas. As children it was the arrival of Santa, the uncle who always brought a good present or the money in the card from Granny. Some of us look forward to the gifts, family gatherings and outings. The people of God had something to look forward to—the blind would see when Christ came, the deaf would hear, shame would be lifted because God is near and creation would be cared for. The poor and the lowly would rejoice. So let's look forward and get a lift in the heart, remembering always those who have little to look forward to—those who pitch their tent in the street, or who just hope the family gathering will be peaceful.

## Reading
*Matthew 8:5–11*

When he entered Capernaum, a centurion came to him, appealing to him and saying, 'Lord, my servant is lying at home paralysed, in terrible distress.' And he said to him, 'I will come and cure him.' The centurion answered, 'Lord, I am not worthy to have you come under my roof; but only speak the word, and my servant will be healed. For I also am a man under authority, with soldiers under me; and I say to one, "Go", and he goes, and to another, "Come", and he comes, and to my slave, "Do this", and the slave does it.' When Jesus heard him, he was amazed and said to those who followed him, 'Truly I tell you, in no one in Israel have I found such faith. I tell you, many will come from east and west and will eat with Abraham and Isaac and Jacob in the kingdom of heaven.'

**Reflect**

In my family, if someone wanted to get you to do something for them, they'd say, usually with a sulk, 'Don't put yourself out.' Of course, you did whatever was asked! This is a lot like the message of the Roman centurion to Jesus. He saw Jesus at work in healing, teaching and praying. Somehow he knew that Jesus could cure the servant even from a distance. He believed that the word of Jesus could reach across the time and the space between people. It wasn't that Jesus didn't want to make the journey. It was, rather, that he wanted to praise the faith of the centurion, a foreigner in Capernaum. Faith is what Jesus looks for, not any restrictive form of religion. Advent is a journey of faith with Jesus to the Bethlehem of our hearts.

**Talk to God**

- Dear God, I pray to see the world as you do. Shine the light of grace and truth into my heart, so that I can see myself and my failings with your merciful eyes. As Advent begins, I ask for the graces that I need and desire at this time.

- I spend some time quietly allowing God's word to take root and become flesh in me.

## Session 2
### Invitation to Stillness
Come into God's presence, knowing that God is already here, waiting for you. Find a comfortable sitting position, slow your breathing, and gradually let go of any tensions in your body, allowing the muscles to relax from your head, neck and face all down your spine and through your lower body to your feet. Let the stillness take over and lead you to a space where you can make room for the God of dreams to be with you.

### Reading
*Isaiah 40:1–11*

> Comfort, O comfort my people,
>    says your God.
> Speak tenderly to Jerusalem,
>    and cry to her
> that she has served her term,
>    that her penalty is paid,
> that she has received from the Lord's hand
>    double for all her sins.
>
> A voice cries out:
> 'In the wilderness prepare the way of the Lord,
>    make straight in the desert a highway for
>       our God.

Every valley shall be lifted up,
> and every mountain and hill be made low;
the uneven ground shall become level,
> and the rough places a plain.
Then the glory of the LORD shall be revealed,
> and all people shall see it together,
>> for the mouth of the LORD has spoken.'

A voice says, 'Cry out!'
> And I said, 'What shall I cry?'
All people are grass,
> their constancy is like the flower of the
>> field.
The grass withers, the flower fades,
> when the breath of the LORD blows upon it;
>> surely the people are grass.
The grass withers, the flower fades;
> but the word of our God will stand for ever.
Get you up to a high mountain,
> O Zion, herald of good tidings;
lift up your voice with strength,
> O Jerusalem, herald of good tidings,
>> lift it up, do not fear;
say to the cities of Judah,
> 'Here is your God!'
See, the Lord GOD comes with might,
> and his arm rules for him;

his reward is with him,
>and his recompense before him.
He will feed his flock like a shepherd;
>he will gather the lambs in his arms,
and carry them in his bosom,
>and gently lead the mother sheep.

## Reflect

Sheep and shepherd are common biblical images. There are many ways to understand these images, but with Jesus the emphasis is very much on the care of the shepherd for the sheep, knowing them almost by name. The shepherd is the one who actively looks after them, especially the lost one. The crook of the shepherd was to lift the sheep out of the briars where they might have fallen. The meaning of Advent is very much about God's care for the people he created out of love. This is the good news that the prophet must shout from the well-known hilltops of Israel.

## Reading

*Matthew 7:21, 24–27*

'Not everyone who says to me, "Lord, Lord", will enter the kingdom of heaven, but only one who does the will of my Father in heaven. . . .

'Everyone then who hears these words of mine and acts on them will be like a wise man who built his house on rock. The rain fell, the floods came, and the winds blew and beat on that house, but it did not fall, because it had been founded on rock. And everyone who hears these words of mine and does not act on them will be like a foolish man who built his house on sand. The rain fell, and the floods came, and the winds blew and beat against that house, and it fell— and great was its fall!'

## Reflect

Some houses were built on a large area of wetland. As a few years went on the occupiers realised that there was a lot of damp coming through the foundations. Something like this reminds us of Jesus' homely advice to build a house on rock rather than sand, or, as the people above might say, on wetlands. Times when we are ill or unemployed make us think of what we build our lives on. The rock Jesus suggests is the faithfulness and love of God. It is trying to make real our words, 'Thy kingdom come, thy will be done'.

**Talk to God**

- This has been another difficult, precarious year. What has helped me to feel safe and secure, settled in my own place? Perhaps I have held on even tighter to my securities? Or perhaps I have sometimes listened to another call, a still, small voice inviting me to live other choices and different relationships? Can I listen to that voice now, in the silence?

- Jesus says, 'Where your treasure is, there will your heart be also'. What gives me a sense of power and status? What makes me feel fragile and vulnerable? As I take time to be still, I share with God my desires and anxieties, my dreads and my dreams.

## Session 3

### Invitation to Stillness

As you come into this time of prayer and reflection, allow your senses to lead you into stillness. Can you hear the sounds outside the room? Inside the room? Perhaps you can smell the scent of a burning candle, feel the warmth of the room protecting you from the cold outside. Let your senses draw you in to the present moment and the presence of our Creator.

### Reading

*Jeremiah 23:5–8*

The days are surely coming, says the LORD, when I will raise up for David a righteous Branch, and he shall reign as king and deal wisely, and shall execute justice and righteousness in the land. In his days Judah will be saved and Israel will live in safety. And this is the name by which he will be called: 'The LORD is our righteousness.'

Therefore, the days are surely coming, says the LORD, when it shall no longer be said, 'As the LORD lives who brought the people of Israel up out of the land of Egypt', but 'As the LORD lives who brought out and led the offspring of the house of Israel out of the land of the north and out of all the lands where he had driven them.' Then they shall live in their own land.

## Reflect

People read this passage for years awaiting the coming of the Messiah. They knew he would come but did not know how. At one time they thought he might be a warrior king, but they knew he was the one who had saved them already and would save them, leading them to a bright future. He would be 'the Lord in our integrity'—the one who would keep his promises. Because of Jesus we too want to be faithful to loved ones. We too want to be people who keep our promises in life—the sign of a life of integrity. Advent reminds us not only of the promises of God but of our promises to God.

## Reading
*Luke 5:17–26*

One day, while he was teaching, Pharisees and teachers of the law were sitting nearby (they had come from every village of Galilee and Judea and from Jerusalem); and the power of the Lord was with him to heal. Just then some men came, carrying a paralysed man on a bed. They were trying to bring him in and lay him before Jesus; but finding no way to bring him in because of the crowd, they went up on the roof and let him down with his bed through the tiles into the middle of the crowd in front of Jesus. When he saw their faith, he said, 'Friend, your sins are forgiven you.' Then the scribes and the Pharisees began to question, 'Who is this who is speaking blasphemies? Who can forgive sins but God alone?' When Jesus perceived their questionings, he answered them, 'Why do you raise such questions in your hearts? Which is easier, to say, "Your sins are forgiven you", or to say, "Stand up and walk"? But so that you may know that the Son of Man has authority on earth to forgive sins'—he said to the one who was paralysed—'I say to you, stand up and take your bed and go to your home.' Immediately he stood up before them, took what he had been lying on, and went to his home, glorifying God. Amazement seized all of them, and they glorified God and were filled with awe, saying, 'We have seen strange things today.'

## Reflect

They saw strange things, the people who were there for the visit of Jesus. They saw a roof being stripped and a stretcher let down in front of Jesus. They witnessed a dispute with religious leaders. They heard that sins were forgiven, and they saw a disabled man walk again. He was amazed too, and the stretcher he brought home would be a permanent souvenir of the best day of his life—the day he met Jesus. Jesus always has something to offer. Anytime we pray, we are the better for it. In meeting him there is healing of the soul, of griefs and hurts and the forgiveness of sins. Christmas and our preparation for it is a time of peace, joy, hope and of the total forgiveness of God.

## Talk to God

- Dear God, open my heart in welcome and remove the obstacles that prevent me receiving Christ with joy.

- Thank you, Lord, for the forgiveness of sin and for healing the effects of sin. I pray for your grace to strengthen me in living a Christian life.

- I ask for peace for my family, friends and all your people; peace of mind and heart, and peace to the world.

## Session 4

### Invitation to Stillness

As you prepare yourself for this time of reflection, call to mind any concerns you have been carrying recently. As you breathe out, share them with God. You might even be able to hand over some of these concerns, at least for now. As you breathe out, hand them over to God. Each time you breathe in, breathe in God's love for you . . . let it fill your body. Take three deeper breaths, keeping this up until you are calm and focused.

### Reading

*Numbers 24:2–7, 15–17*

Balaam looked up and saw Israel camping tribe by tribe. Then the spirit of God came upon him, and he uttered his oracle, saying:

> 'The oracle of Balaam son of Beor,
>> the oracle of the man whose eye is clear,
> the oracle of one who hears the words of God,
>> who sees the vision of the Almighty,
>> who falls down, but with eyes uncovered:
> how fair are your tents, O Jacob,
>> your encampments, O Israel!
> Like palm groves that stretch far away,
>> like gardens beside a river,

like aloes that the LORD has planted,
  like cedar trees beside the waters.
Water shall flow from his buckets,
  and his seed shall have abundant water,
his king shall be higher than Agag,
  and his kingdom shall be exalted. . . .

So he uttered his oracle, saying:

'The oracle of Balaam son of Beor,
  the oracle of the man whose eye is clear,
the oracle of one who hears the words of God,
  and knows the knowledge of the Most High,
who sees the vision of the Almighty,
  who falls down, but with his eyes
      uncovered:
I see him, but not now;
  I behold him, but not near—
a star shall come out of Jacob,
  and a sceptre shall rise out of Israel;
it shall crush the borderlands of Moab,
  and the territory of all the Shethites.'

**Reflect**

Balaam's poems are poems of faith. He cannot see
what he believes in: 'I see him now, but not in the
present'. He was a patient waiter, both waiting for his

Saviour to come and waiting to speak to his people the word of God. In Advent we know what we are waiting for, but we know the one we are waiting for will come in his own time. Much of life is about waiting, whether it is for growth, love, happiness or health. We wait for God in many ways: in our prayer and our wondering about who and what God is. We never come to the end of waiting, but times like Christmas increase our faith that the good things of God are around the corner. We wait also knowing that in all of our lives God has good things in store for us.

## Reading
### Matthew 1:18–24

Now the birth of Jesus the Messiah took place in this way. When his mother Mary had been engaged to Joseph, but before they lived together, she was found to be with child from the Holy Spirit. Her husband Joseph, being a righteous man and unwilling to expose her to public disgrace, planned to dismiss her quietly. But just when he had resolved to do this, an angel of the Lord appeared to him in a dream and said, 'Joseph, son of David, do not be afraid to take Mary as your wife, for the child conceived in her is from the Holy Spirit. She will bear a son, and you are to name him Jesus, for he will save his people from their sins.' All this took place to fulfil what had been spoken by the Lord through the prophet:

> 'Look, the virgin shall conceive and bear a son,
>     and they shall name him Emmanuel',

which means, 'God is with us.' When Joseph awoke from sleep, he did as the angel of the Lord commanded him; he took her as his wife.

## Reflect

The Messiah came in an unexpected way. He came as a baby in the womb of a woman who was engaged to be married. He came as a baby conceived through the Holy Spirit of God. It's a bit the same today. God comes to us in unusual and surprising ways: in a moment of unexpected prayer, in the love and support of a spouse, partner or friend; in the beauty of creation, in the words of the Scripture. God is with us even when we struggle. Advent gives us time to allow this to happen. Then we will recognise the Lord as a special presence at Christmas.

**Talk to God**

- I turn my attention to Christ's life for a moment. A baby was born in a simple stable into a suffering world. He lived a life in service of the suffering, before suffering for us on a cross. I spend some time sitting now with Jesus, who has experienced the very depths of suffering.

- Dear God, I pray for those who are suffering in the world today. I ask for a clear sense of how I can help those around me who are in poverty, pain or despair.

# Conclusion

As this Advent Retreat comes to an end, take time to reflect on what stays with you from this special time of prayer. How was your heart moved during this time? Has any scripture passage remained with you? Did you find yourself struggling at any point, or resisting the words and meaning of the scriptures you read? Have you received any graces? Can you see a change in yourself? What did you find difficult or challenging? Perhaps it would be helpful to write down any new insights you have received, or any ideas for new beginnings that have come to light.

Ask Jesus to help you see all that you have been blessed with and to hold on to any graces you have received. Take some time to thank God for this sacred time you have spent together and for the deepening of your relationship. Perhaps you could resolve to take some new steps every day to continue to nurture the relationship. Perhaps this Christmas you can offer God the gift of your time and attention as you continue on the road to Bethlehem with Jesus Emmanuel, God-with-us. Come, Lord Jesus.